HENRY THE HELICOPTER HAS ONE PROPELLER

Retold by NICHOLAS IAN

Illustrated by DIEGO FUNCK

Music Produced by ERIK KOSKINEN and
Recorded at REAL PHONIC STUDIOS

CANTATA
LEARNING

WWW.CANTATALEARNING.COM

CANTATA LEARNING

Published by Cantata Learning
1710 Roe Crest Drive
North Mankato, MN 56003
www.cantatalearning.com

A note to educators and librarians from the publisher: Cantata Learning has provided the following data to assist in book processing and suggested use of Cantata Learning product.

Publisher's Cataloging-in-Publication Data
Prepared by Librarian Consultant: Ann-Marie Begnaud
Library of Congress Control Number: 2015958167
    Henry the Helicopter Has One Propeller
    Series: Tangled Tunes : On the Move
    Retold by Nicholas Ian
    Illustrated by Diego Funck
    Summary: Sing about the different vehicles you see around town in this twist on a classic song.
    ISBN: 978-1-63290-615-1 (library binding/CD)
    ISBN: 978-1-63290-630-4 (paperback/CD)
Suggested Dewey and Subject Headings:
    Dewey: E 388
    LCSH Subject Headings: Transportation – Juvenile literature. | Counting – Juvenile literature. | Transportation – Songs and music – Texts. | Counting – Songs and music – Texts. | Transportation – Juvenile sound recordings. | Counting – Juvenile sound recordings.
    Sears Subject Headings: Transportation. | Counting. | School songbooks. | Children's songs. | Folk music.
    BISAC Subject Headings: JUVENILE NONFICTION / Transportation / General. | JUVENILE NONFICTION / Music / Songbooks. | JUVENILE NONFICTION / Concepts / Counting & Numbers.

Book design and art direction, Tim Palin Creative
Editorial direction, Flat Sole Studio
Music direction, Elizabeth Draper
Music produced by Erik Koskinen and recorded at Real Phonic Studios

Printed in the United States of America in North Mankato, Minnesota.
072016   0335CGF16

Vehicles are all around us. Some drive along streets. Others fly through the air. Count their wheels, horns, doors, and lights before they zoom away.

Now turn the page and sing along!

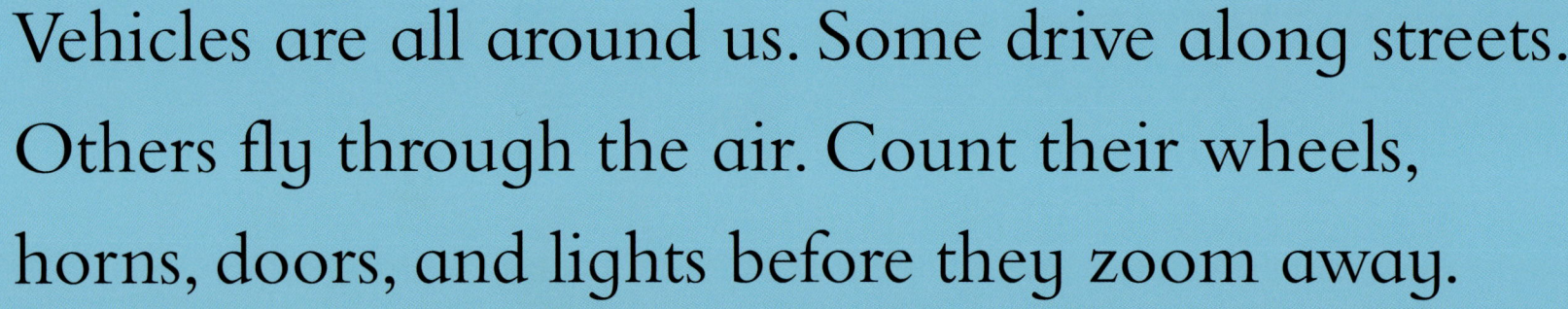

Henry the helicopter has one **propeller**.

Henry the helicopter has one propeller.

Henry the helicopter has one propeller.

Go, helicopter. Go!

Mary the motorcycle has two wheels.

Mary the motorcycle has two wheels.

Mary the motorcycle has two wheels.

Go, motorcycle. Go!

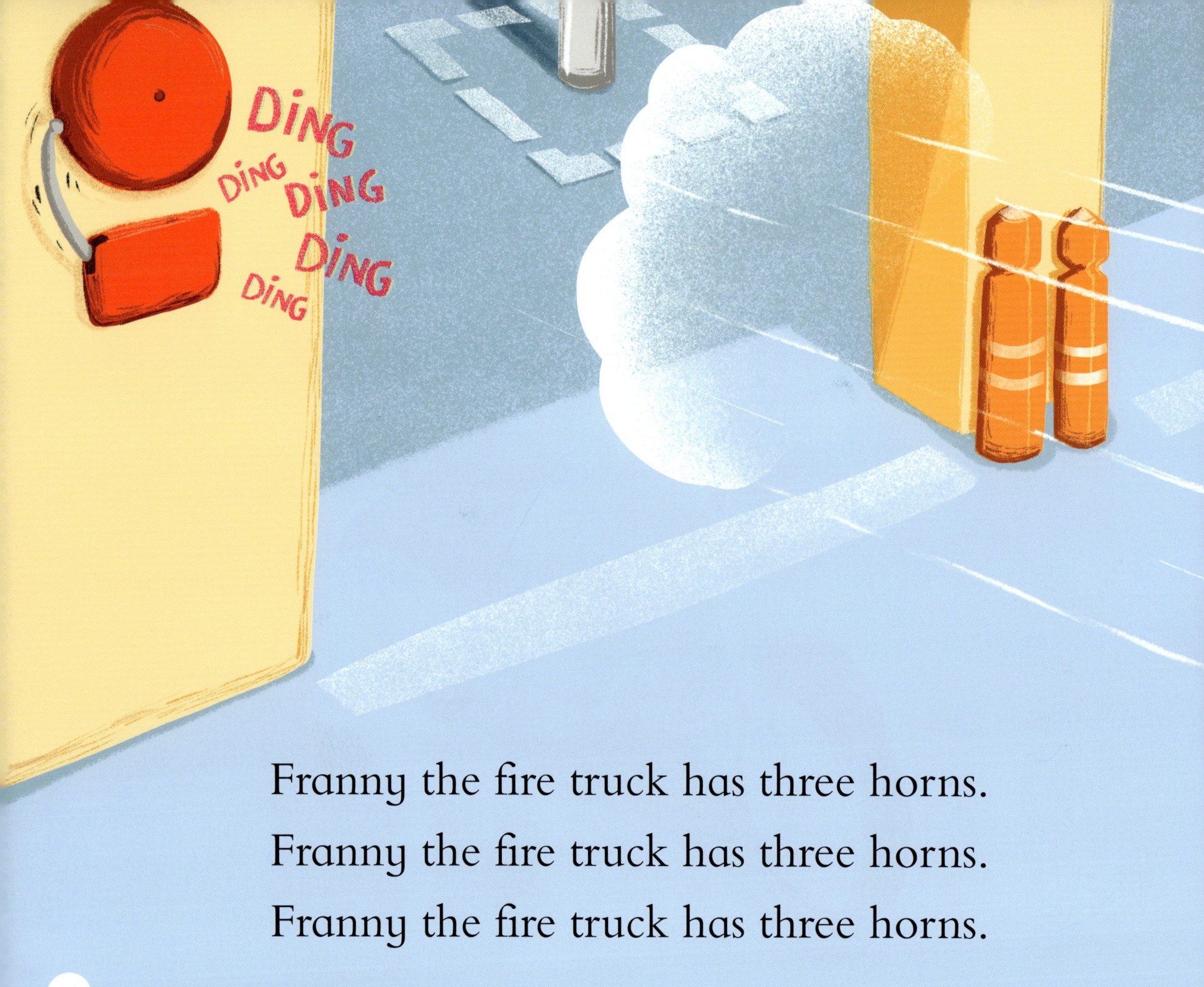

Franny the fire truck has three horns.

Franny the fire truck has three horns.

Franny the fire truck has three horns.

Go, fire truck. Go!

Tommy the **taxicab** has four doors.
Tommy the taxicab has four doors.
Tommy the taxicab has four doors.

Go, taxicab. Go!

Patty the police car has five lights.
Patty the police car has five lights.
Patty the police car has five lights.

Go, police car. Go!

Danny the dump truck has four mirrors.

Danny the dump truck has four mirrors.

Danny the dump truck has four mirrors.

Go, dump truck. Go!

Tony the tricycle has three wheels.

Tony the tricycle has three wheels.

Tony the tricycle has three wheels.

Go, tricycle. Go!

Annie the airplane has two wings.

Annie the airplane has two wings.

Annie the airplane has two wings.

Go, airplane. Go!

Sally the semitruck has one horn.
Sally the semitruck has one horn.
Sally the semitruck has one horn.

Go, semitruck. Go!

SONG LYRICS

Henry the Helicopter Has One Propeller

Henry the helicopter has one propeller.
Henry the helicopter has one propeller.
Henry the helicopter has one propeller.
Go, helicopter. Go!

Mary the motorcycle has two wheels.
Mary the motorcycle has two wheels.
Mary the motorcycle has two wheels.
Go, motorcycle. Go!

Franny the fire truck has three horns.
Franny the fire truck has three horns.
Franny the fire truck has three horns.
Go, fire truck. Go!

Tommy the taxicab has four doors.
Tommy the taxicab has four doors.
Tommy the taxicab has four doors.
Go, taxicab. Go!

Patty the police car has five lights.
Patty the police car has five lights.
Patty the police car has five lights.
Go, police car. Go!

Danny the dump truck has four mirrors.
Danny the dump truck has four mirrors.
Danny the dump truck has four mirrors.
Go, dump truck. Go!

Tony the tricycle has three wheels.
Tony the tricycle has three wheels.
Tony the tricycle has three wheels.
Go, tricycle. Go!

Annie the airplane has two wings.
Annie the airplane has two wings.
Annie the airplane has two wings.
Go, airplane. Go!

Sally the semitruck has one horn.
Sally the semitruck has one horn.
Sally the semitruck has one horn.
Go, semitruck. Go!

Henry the Helicopter Has One Propeller

Americana
Erik Koskinen

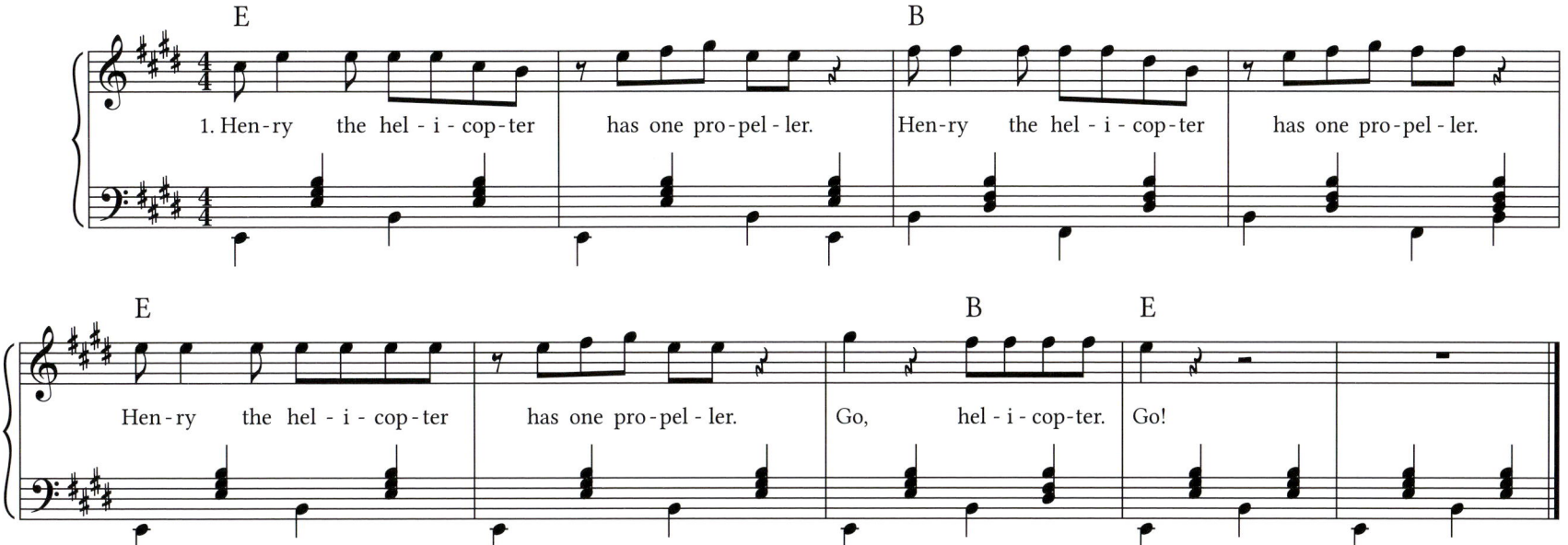

Verse 2
Mary the motorcycle has two wheels.
Mary the motorcycle has two wheels.
Mary the motorcycle has two wheels.
Go, motorcycle. Go!

Verse 3
Franny the fire truck has three horns.
Franny the fire truck has three horns.
Franny the fire truck has three horns.
Go, fire truck. Go!

Verse 4
Tommy the taxicab has four doors.
Tommy the taxicab has four doors.
Tommy the taxicab has four doors.
Go, taxicab. Go!

Verse 5
Patty the police car has five lights.
Patty the police car has five lights.
Patty the police car has five lights.
Go, police car. Go!

Verse 6
Danny the dump truck has four mirrors.
Danny the dump truck has four mirrors.
Danny the dump truck has four mirrors.
Go, dump truck. Go!

Verse 7
Tony the tricycle has three wheels.
Tony the tricycle has three wheels.
Tony the tricycle has three wheels.
Go, tricycle. Go!

Verse 8
Annie the airplane has two wings.
Annie the airplane has two wings.
Annie the airplane has two wings.
Go, airplane. Go!

Verse 9
Sally the semitruck has one horn.
Sally the semitruck has one horn.
Sally the semitruck has one horn.
Go, semitruck. Go!

GLOSSARY

propeller—blades on a vehicle, such as a helicopter, airplane, or boat, that spin and make the vehicle move

taxicab—a car that carries people who pay to ride

GUIDED READING ACTIVITIES

1. How many different vehicles were mentioned in this song? Can you think of any vehicles that were not included?

2. Next time you sing this song, instead of saying the numbers in each verse, hold up that many fingers instead.

3. Draw a picture of your favorite vehicle in this song.

TO LEARN MORE

Abramovitz, Melissa. *Emergency Vehicles*. Mankato, MN: Capstone Press, 2015.

Anderson, Steven. *Wheels on the Bus*. Mankato, MN: Cantata Learning, 2016.

Clay, Kathryn. *Construction Vehicles*. Mankato, MN: Capstone Press, 2015.

Ipcizade, Catherine. *H Is for Honk! A Transportation Alphabet*. Mankato, MN: Capstone Press, 2011.